UNLEARN:

DITCH FAILED MONEY HABITS
AND
DISCOVER FINANCIAL FREEDOM

BY NICOLE JONES

ISBN: 978-1-7350529-0-8
AUTHOR: Nicole Jones
EDITOR: Tawni Fears

DISCLAIMER
I am not a certified financial planner/advisor nor a certified financial analyst, an economist, a CPA, an accountant nor a lawyer. I am not a finance professional through formal education. I am someone who believes in and takes pride in a sense of freedom, satisfaction, fulfillment and empowerment from being financially competent. The contents in this material are for informational purposes only and does not constitute formal financial, accounting, or legal advice. The content shared are personal steps I took to gain financial freedom and therefore sharing my personal journey with others seeking the advice of others. I cannot promise that the information shared will appropriately fit your financial situation or provide the expected results. By using this material, you agree to hold me harmless from any ramifications, financial or otherwise, that occur to you as a result of acting on information.

DEDICATION

All thanks to God for his favor. A special thank you to my husband Greg, for his love and patience.

To those reading this remember, the greatest gift you can give yourself is to follow your goals.

change your mindset because you cannot afford to settle

Nicole Jones

TABLE OF CONTENTS

INTRODUCTION

Have you ever felt like you have a calling on your life to accomplish something powerful? You spend years trying to crack the code and decipher the message towards success. Well if you answered yes, I am right there with you. What I found out is quite often the answer is right in front of you. Those gifts you do so often for other people that just comes naturally to you are the things that will lead you to success. Nurture your God-given gifts. Begin to explore how your natural abilities can help those around you.

So what does this mean concerning the context of this book? No, my natural ability is not keeping a balanced budget or being a financial guru. I find it easy to plan, organize, and be a leader. Whenever there is a new project or idea, I can easily craft an entire launch plan from start to finish. I had to learn how to pair my gifts with things I am not so good at, like money management.

In this book, I will share some of my most personal situations as it relates to finances. These are details I have not shared with anyone other than family and a handful of friends. I find it essential to share these personal accounts because I know I am not alone. This information can help someone else succeed financially. Ultimately, the goal is to encourage every reader that financial freedom is possible, and we have everything we need within us and around us to bring forth generational wealth.

I have learned and still learning that financial freedom has life-changing benefits. To take it a step back, the process in preparation towards liberty is even more rewarding. You are breaking down financial and generational barriers. This unearthed enlightenment can positively influence those around you. You learn more about yourself, both strengths and weaknesses. Be prepared for both and embrace your transformation.

I had to shift my way of thinking and be open to financial management techniques I had never learned. My goal was to pay off student loan debt, increase my savings, invest and build generational wealth. I was not going to be able to achieve that with limited thinking. I knew God had more for me, and I needed to obey His word on my life. So what did I do to discover financial freedom? The chapters that follow outline the entire process, good and bad.

This is your moment to create a legacy, shift your mindset and follow God's plan for your life. We all can elevate our choices and then help those around us do the same. Your financial freedom starts today and will last for generations.

one
rob peter to pay paul

The earliest memory I have with money is receiving multiple one-dollar bills, equaling no more than five or ten bucks. This money bags was typically for my birthday or from the tooth fairy. Those days I thought I was rich, a millionaire even, and that I could buy out the entire candy aisle. Despite being young and the oldest of three, I knew I could not just walk into a store, grab what I wanted, and have the means to afford it. The store lecture was, when we walk in this store, don't touch nothing, don't look at nothing, and don't ask for nothing. As a matter of fact, keep your hands in your pockets.

Growing up in a single-family household, meant money was tight for us. However, the irony is as soon as I got money, I was ready to spend it. In those instances, my great-grandmother used to say, that money burning your hand.

Where did I get this urge to spend? At a young age, I learned when you have money you spend it.
Now thinking back, I am giving myself some grace because I was young. I did not know any better. However, that introduction was only the start of poor money habits later in life.

The only thing I can attribute these habits to would be my financial upbringing. I am incredibly grateful to have both parents in my life. They offered us the tools to succeed and keep God first in all things. We spent amble time with our dad. He provided support in more ways than one and many laughs throughout our life. Ultimately, we grew up in a single-family household and our mom was the one who raised us. She is a giving and hardworking woman and did the best she knew how to provide for three kids, with multiple jobs, and help from our great-grandmother. When payday rolled around, the money was already allocated to responsibilities around the house and rightfully so. At the moment, it did not feel like we were on hard times until it did.

I learned the term "rob Peter to pay Paul" at a very young age when my mom had to determine whether the light or water bill would get paid. As a result, there were evenings my siblings and I played games under candlelight. There were many other scenarios where tough decisions like this had to be made. In the dead of winter, have heat or buy a space heater? Buy gas for the car or get food? Let me take a moment to acknowledge all the single mothers out there making challenging decisions to provide for the family. Lord knows I am beyond grateful for what my mom sacrificed.

She provided everything she could with all that she had. Do not get me wrong, I do not want to paint the picture that every day was a struggle, but there were tough moments. We had plenty of joyous times growing up. We had more good times than bad. It was just money, in my mind and through my eyes, was scarce, and one would always have to decide what to sacrifice. Saving money was a foreign term. It was one of those things I was told to do, but no one really showed me how it is done.

The act of living paycheck to paycheck was normalized. As if it were a rite of passage towards adulthood.

Those instilled financial practices became the way I acted as a young adult. Struggling to make ends meet was familiar. It was all I knew. I did not know how to part from that behavior. I have encountered a number of people who echo the same sentiments as it pertains to financial upbringing. This is not a me scenario, this is a lot of us.

I am extremely grateful that my parents always encouraged us to be great. Without them I would not be where I am today, breaking barriers and sharing my truth. My financial literacy backstory is necessary for providing the full picture of my journey of how I managed to pay off thousands of dollars in student loan debt. To prepare for college I did not have a lot of support through scholarships. Obtaining a bank loan was fairly simple as a seventeen-year-old going into college. One major flag, I had no idea what I was really getting myself into. I did not understand interest or how much the loan would be when I graduated.

The loan officer gave me a brief summary of the student loan process. I eagerly nodded, confirming I heard what was said, but honestly had no idea how to make sense of it all. It all sounded like gibberish. I was more enamored with the fact I was going to college and this was my lottery ticket to get there. There I was young, excited, but unaware of the financial outcome. I had a loan before I had my driver's license.

My financial decisions as a young adult are a cumulation of past financial habits and understandings. Money discussions around the dinner table was not a thing. Student loan elimination did not all happen at one time. An increased savings account did not occur overnight. Involvement with investments was not a natural conversation. For me, understanding this part of my life as the root of my financial relationship with money was critical. How else would I be able to identify my money issues? Thinking back on my financial history helped shape my financial roadmap.

REFLECTION
What did you learn about money growing up with your family?
How do you feel about banks making the loan request process so easy for teenagers to obtain?
What should our rising college students understand before obtaining a loan?
What financial habits do you need to let go of now?
List three steps of action you should do to let go of financial complacency.

two
how to flip $50k

Fast-forward to May 2013 when I graduated from Georgia State University. That was one of the best moments of my life! I learned so much about myself during those years of development. I partied many nights, studied until the crack of dawn, and secured internships. I had accomplished a lot in college and failed some too. I changed my major, found out I was taking the wrong course after the semester, flunked math twice, and lost the Hope Scholarship. Adapting to the city life came with a price, and my loan for living in downtown Atlanta and school tuition was adding up quickly.

A lot happened in those six years of college, including taking out hefty student loans to afford school and books. Also, in my first year, I lived downtown off-campus, which was pricey. Between private loans and federal loans after graduation, I was in the hole $59,716.68.

What also went wrong? Refund checks! They were a disaster for my financial relationship. Outside of buying used books, that money went right to Lenox Mall, parties, family, and unnecessary things. Before I had the money, I was already spending it in my head. Those funds were used irresponsibly. I was not practical about needs or the future.

I regret the fact that I did not ask more questions when applying for loans. What went wrong was my lack of knowledge. I did not take financial literacy into my own hands. Instead, I lacked financial responsibility. I had thousands of dollars in the bank account and still broke. A broken money mindset was in full control. The sad thing is, after a few blow money fast moments, I distinctly remember feeling like I did not spend money wisely. Every semester the refund check was depleted. Each semester, I told myself I would save a certain amount. And then, each semester, I had nothing to show for it. What was previously described is the definition of insanity. Saying you are going to do one thing, but still producing the same results. I kept telling myself I would do better next refund check. Then, I would not. Instead, I would get close to the end of the funds and simply blow it. Eating out all the time, buying clothes, and everything else in between that you can imagine.

It was when I entered my career after college that I realized a poor person could gain a lot of cash and could still be broke. I was the prime example. Here I was young and frivolous. I had more money than I had in my life, earning $50,000 salary with a take home of $20,000 after taxes; also considering I joined job late in the year.

I continued to find myself back at square one without a dollar to my name. More money does not make you wealthy, good money habits do. Before the student loan debt, I was already in a deficit. I was already operating from a place of meager means. The main issue was I lacked financial literacy. Honestly, at the time, I did not know where to pinpoint my financial struggles. When you are accustomed to functioning a certain way, you cannot see beyond the what is in front you. You stick to what you know only because it is comfortable. Once I graduated, I had a significantly ugly debt over my head. It was like a label identifying me as someone with no understanding of finances.

How do you flip $50k? You do exactly what I did. I was able to flip the loan, but not in the way I needed it to. Due to my lack of understanding it turned into more debt. Moreover, I missed payments, and in other instances did not pay enough once the loan repayment started months into the repayment stage. That only caused the loans to skyrocket in interest and overall balance. Once all was said and done, I was $80,398 in debt. There is an embarrassing story about how I realized my real debt later. There I was with all that debt before turning twenty-five. More on this in the next chapter. Ultimately, I knew something had to change.

REFLECTION
What is your ugly number?
What are some factors that led you to this debt?
Are you ready to commit to changing your mindset, habits, and financial situation?

three
houston we have a problem

Three months after college graduation and I had my first job. I am sure I am not the first to tell you this, but it is a job finding a job. I made a wish list of my top interests, then the top companies I wanted to work for (in and outside of Atlanta) that met those interests, and finally sought out their job portal and applied to every job that matched my ideal job description. Those three months felt like an eternity, but I am grateful God saw it fit for me. There I was, working a corporate job as a communications specialist with a salary of $50,000 and benefits in a high-rise office in downtown Atlanta. At that moment, I knew I was winning at #adulting. Everything felt like it was on the up and up from there.

Immediately, I began contributing to my 401k at the company match. To keep it real, I did not know all the ins-and-outs of this investment, but I knew it was important for my future. Therefore, I did what I could.

Contributing to a 401k was just one of those things I heard about and honestly did not grasp the entire scope of it all, but either way I made it a point to commit. Another reason I wanted to set this up ASAP is because, knowing myself, I did not want to pocket that money. Or should I say spend it?

With all the thrill of starting my first career job, I could have quickly fallen into being comfortable with the additional money and abusing the situation. Much like the refund check that was provided in college, any extra money would have been subject to excessive spending. I had enough sense to know a 401k is essential, and since I could contribute, I exercised that right. I would say that was my most mature money moment during that time.

Broke and Confused

There is a six-month grace period after graduation before student loan repayment activates. As soon as that time approached, I truly felt what it meant to live paycheck to paycheck. Prior to the grace period, my take-home income felt like it came in and went right back out the door. I did not have a lot of bills. I had my phone bill, helped my mom with bills, and now my student loan debt. But with those few items it felt like money just evaporated. Now with student loan payments in the mix it reflected how bad off I really was with money. Student loan payments equaled 50% of my monthly take home. However, I did not allow that to stop me. I still found myself trying to be involved in happy hours and shopping. There were several times I skipped student loan payments or did not pay the full monthly amount because I wanted to use the money elsewhere. That caused interest in the loan to increase drastically!

Here I was with a full-time salaried job and received more insufficient funds notifications than I did without a job. I felt broke and confused. I questioned how I would make it on the journey to adulthood. How would I ever move out of my mom's house? How would I ever be able to save any money? How did I expect to tithe more at church? I felt like a fraud. I was a seemingly put-together person with an ideal job situation after college. Only to find myself struggling to keep a few dollars in my bank account. There were no more refund checks to help me bounce back mid-semester. I was succeeding publicly professionally and failing in silence financially.

Financial Bondage
Have you dealt with imposter syndrome? Feel like everyone views your life as perfect, but deep down you know there are quite a few skeletons in the closet? Poor financial management can be a silent killer if you let it. It can fester into your daily life, cause you frustration and bring unwanted stress. That was me. Some days, money was the first thing I thought about waking up. Trying to figure out how I was going to pay a bill. Not only did I have to change my behavior, but my thoughts. I had limiting beliefs. I could not see past what I had and continuously thought in a broke mentality. My energy and thoughts were giving off broken beliefs. It was a haunting feeling and I vowed I did not want to feel that ever again. I had to break this financial bondage and repair my outlook on managing money. I lacked self-discipline and needed to do something about it. If this speaks to you, I encourage you to stop your current financial habits. You do not need to spiral any longer down a hole of debt and disappointment. There is hope for you.

Open your mind to new ways of financial thinking. Tackle what you can by using the budget spreadsheet in the reference section. Do not think as I did with limits and scarcity. I was operating in way that narrowly focused on immediate needs and not long-term gains; which continuously left me with little to no money. Exploring a more optimistic approach towards money will attract a positive outcome. Thoughts of how can I better serve myself, my household and the community with more cashflow are healthy. Luxurious thoughts are also great, but think of how you can sustain wealth not only for you, but generations to come. Change your thoughts to abundance and not limits.

REFLECTION
Ever felt like you are struggling with imposter syndrome? How do you cope with doubt and defeat?
Who are the positive people in your life you can go to even when the road gets tough?
What limiting beliefs do you need to let go of?

four
true partnership

Prior to dating, Greg and I were friends always discussing ways to elevate our careers, our ambitions and ways to build a stable life. Eventually our friendship progressed until we became inseparable. Our discussions about the future, being a power couple, and following our dreams continued. For our relationship to continue to take flight, I needed to share more about my financial woes. I needed help in figuring out better practices. Greg is much better with financial management than me, so I knew I could go to him in confidence.

His natural ability to make complex subjects simple is such a great skill of his. It was through his coaching later in our marriage that I learned how to trade the stock market, but we will get to that later. In a matter of several months after the start of loan payback, I found myself closer to the $80,000 mark.

That came as a result of late payments and a lack of payments. The accrued interest was stacked higher than I could imagine. For whatever reason, I thought paying an extra $10 here or $50 there would help bring down the payments. I was wrong! The poor man's formula I had been executing did not warrant progress. Instead, debt continued to pile on thick.

With Greg's guidance, I was able to face this big, hairy, ugly monster called debt. Remember that embarrassing moment I mentioned earlier? Well here it goes. We reviewed my student loan debt, my monthly income, and expenses. Mind you, it was only during this exercise did I realize I was more like $80,398 in debt! I kept reciting; it is close to $60,000. Maybe it was wishful thinking, lack of understanding, or a combination of both. Either way, the number was fictitious, and once we reviewed everything, it was clear. Yeah, at one point, I was close to $60,000 ($59,716.68 to be exact). But again, my lack of financial knowledge was hurting me. I was much deeper in the hole.

What did we do? We put a plan in place, and over the years, the plan shifted based on new income and new ways to tackle debt. This plan, in the form of a spreadsheet, incorporated daily spending as well. We made it a requirement to have monthly financial check-ins for both of our spending habits. I am not going to lie; those conversations were uncomfortable. I never really talked through my spending at this level of detail with anyone. We then took this data and identified where we needed to improve and sacrifice.

Here are the categories used for our plan:

- Home bills
- Daily expenses
- Transportation
- Travel
- Entertainment
- Health
- Recreation
- Subscriptions
- Personal
- Financial obligations
- Miscellaneous
- Income

A snapshot of this spreadsheet is available in the reference section. It is actually the same financial model used starting in 2013 all the way to debt freedom in 2020. Our first review of finances I clearly identified student loans was not my only issue. I had a problem with dining out, coffee runs, and buying things beyond my means. Here is the thing I had to unlearn everything I knew about financial management. Learning the fundamentals of money management was half the battle. I had to also be open to change, shift my mindset, and sacrifice.

What is also key to this process? Greg was my helpmate. Again, this is all while in the dating phase. No joint account or help with payments, just guidance. We got through this together without judgment. If anything, I was harder on myself during this process. I felt like a failure and stupid. I cried because of the level of embarrassment.

Greg was patient and saw the light at the end of the tunnel. We got married in 2016 and have separate and joint accounts. I still made the necessary payments towards student loans from personal my income.

In your financial journey find your helpmate, whether that is a family member or friend who has their finances in order or a financial advisor. Having that support person provides you accountability that will lead you closer to your goals. When it comes to relationships and money, having open lines of communication is critical. As we know, the main reasons marriages lead to divorce is because of money and communication. While we were dating, we were tackling both. Whether you are dating or married, talk through your finances. Discuss topics like:

- What are your financial goals?
- What financial struggles are you facing?
- What money management lessons did you learn growing up?
- What do you want to learn more about regarding money?
- What do you invest in or would like to invest in?
- What debt are your trying to eliminate?
- What are your thoughts about generational wealth?
- How can we help each other be successful in our financial goals?

Be open in your conversations, hear each other out, and learn more about each other's goals. Even if you are single share these questions with family or friends. These questions are meant to disrupt and eliminate the idea that talking about money is a taboo subject.

REFLECTION

Who is your helpmate, and how can you continue to encourage each other?

When was the last time you two sat down to dig into your finances?

What new financial habits do you two need to create together?

five
no more excuses

Like I mentioned before, I needed to create a relationship with money. Greg served as my money therapist to help me establish this newfound relationship with money. For him to get me in shape, there was one thing I had to do first. Remove my ego! As I was getting help, I found myself trying to justify and defend every expense. I needed to remove this shell protecting my habits. I came up with every excuse as to why I needed yet another business suit for work or why I had to spend $50 at happy hour. I tried to justify every dollar spent and why it was necessary. In reality, I was making irresponsible decisions with money. I was so upset that I was not making enough in my new job and that I was living paycheck to paycheck only to realize I was the issue. I did not know what balancing a bank account meant. I identified my relationship with money as complicated, not because I did not have enough, yet I did not know how to manage it.

No longer could I blame my failed attempts of managing money on my upbringing and lack of knowledge. I had to change my way of thinking. I had to unlearn what I thought I knew about finances. I had to sacrifice what I thought were dire needs. I had to activate self-discipline. There was a lot on the to-do list that required self-reflection and determination. I honestly had to break down my notion of money and build it back up again. That was the only way I was going to eliminate student loan debt and manage my money better.

To make it plain, this is a difficult step. It was for me, anyway. Even though I sought help, I had to make a mindset shift. It was uncomfortable. I felt agitated. You have to get out of your way when it comes to improving your financial situation. When you do not have your finances in order, the topic of personal finance, when seeking guidance from others, can sometimes feel like an attack. It can feel as though you are being scrutinized for your spending decisions. Acknowledge the fact that you have to reframe your thinking because it is really more of an assessment. Whether you are seeking the help of a financial advisor or someone close that has their finances in order, they are here to assist you.

REFLECTION
What financial excuses will you stop today?
It is okay to ask for help, who will you reach out to help you get your finances in order?
Do you compare your financial situation to others? That ends today! Create your own financial success metric.

six
debt eliminators

There is no one way to eliminate debt in my book (see what I did there). For me to reach this milestone, I had to practice multiple tactics. Here are the top four ways I was able to eliminate debt and can help you too:

- Created a budget plan
- Mapped out ways to get a salary increase
- Remained consistently faithful
- Applied to refinance my loans

Budget Plan
Creating a budget plan and putting all my numbers on one sheet opened my eyes. I was so lost in what I thought I knew about my bills and income. Until I had a spreadsheet with everything in front of me, I further realized I had no idea what I was doing. You must know your numbers! I consistently made inadequate assessments with my money; hence, why student loan debt grew astronomically.

Budgeting allows you to organize your money and have a smart spending plan. It will enable you to have enough money for what you need, save, and ultimately eliminate debt. Not only did budgeting help me keep more money in my account without over drafting, but I was also able to create a savings account.

Before that point here is how my savings account worked:

- Received paycheck
- Moved money into savings
- Paid bills
- Spent money on essentials
- Spent money on nonessentials
- More nonessentials
- Overdraft
- Move savings to checking
- If I did not have cash in savings, then ask parents for money
- Repeat

Over time, I was able to save more by cutting back on expenses and not tap into that account consistently. That was a massive milestone for me. I felt empowered and accomplished. The act of paying myself first made me happy. It brought a level of assurance and security. If you have never had a budget plan, initially, it can be challenging to follow. You must change your thoughts, behavior, and overall mindset. If you are anything like me, you might need to limit outings.

As much as I loved hanging out with friends at all the new foodie locations. I had to decline quite a few to get my finances in order. Accept that you need to make a difference in your lifestyle first to see an increase in your funds. Once you get over this hurdle, you will begin to see results.

In the reference section, I provide a snapshot of the monthly budget plan I used to start my financial freedom process.

What is vital to point out here is be sure to outline every expense. That allows you to see the landscape of your finances and where you need to trim spending. That will tell you exactly where all your money is going. Remember in Chapter 3, I mentioned I felt like I was living paycheck to paycheck? Well, this spreadsheet revealed it was not because I was not making enough; it was my spending habits. I am not going to lie, by consistently using this spreadsheet I did not all sudden enjoy financial management. Math is still NOT my favorite subject. However, being more educated about how money works is essential to making wise choices.

Salary Leaps
Over time, I realized I would not be able to eliminate debt and save any more than I had been without seeking an increase in salary. Another stream of income was an idea, but not the route I could manage at the time. What I could control was my career path and the trajectory I saw for myself. I decided to educate myself on ways to improve my skills on the job. At an entry-level position, I had room to grow in the industry of project management.

I made a switch from a communications specialist to a project coordinator. This moved me from $50,000 up to a $54,000 salary. Since, I have made more financial leaps in my career. What also helped was the company paid for educational courses to excel, and I took advantage of the opportunity.

It was that first course that sparked something in me always to negotiate educational credit as part of my hiring package when stepping into a new role. I encourage you to always negotiate what is important to you during the hiring process. Education is your key to advancement in your career and life. Seek out opportunities to grow in your career. Reach out to your manager or human resources to inquire about funded certifications. Even if you do not see anything publicly posted about it in your workplace, I encourage you to inquire still. As you move up in your career or make a career shift, do not leave money on the table. Negotiate your worth in comparison to the average salary of the role. You know based on your education and experience, what you should earn. When my salary increased, more money was allocated to student loan debt. With the budget plan, I was able to see the debt chisel away month over month.

Consistently Faithful

What is funny about the budget plan created years ago was the student debt target completion. Based on how much I was originally paying on the loan we mapped out the expected completion would be 2025. Immediately, that did not sit well with me. My first response was, Oh, no! I am going to complete that before I turn 35.

I was convinced that it would happen. At the time, I did not know how the heck I was going to do it. Call it faith! I just knew it was not going to carry into my mid-thirties. At thirty-one years old and I am DONE with student loan debt! God will make a way! Even when you cannot see things moving in the direction you want, just know God is working behind the scenes setting you up for success. Before you know it, your faith will bear the fruits you have consistently watered.

Whether it is your faith or reaching a goal, you must remain consistent in your practice. My goal was to eliminate student loan debt and improve my overall financial situation. I had to commit to a budget, a timeline, and a strategy to reach success. There were several times I questioned God. Why do I not have a more substantial salary? How was I going to make ends meet with so little money? In those moments, life felt hard, and I felt like a failure. I was asking the wrong questions. See the gag was, God was not going to provide me with an increase when I could not handle what I had. Why would God provide me with an extra $1000 if I could not manage $100? I had to change my mindset and behavior. What I should have asked initially, God, how can I best manage my finances so that it is pleasing to you and the plan you have for my life?

Even in what I would consider a dark place in my finances, I began to tithe. Even if that only left me $50 in my checking account. I tithe consistently. It was not always 10%, but it was to ensure I was giving to the most high. Situations began to turn around for the good the more consistent I became tithing.

There is power in being obedient to God's will. When I become more consistent it was as though money would appear out of nowhere. I couldn't explain why it got to the point where I was finding money or I got credited back money. Overall, everything seemed to progress in the right direction and I started to become less of a slave to money and more of a money magnet. A few times, I fell off tithing, and it showed. Money began to take a turn for the worst. Financially things became rocky. In general, I had to ensure my spiritual foundation was solid. I had to make sure I was not only committed to His purpose in my life, but also made my necessary contribution. Whatever your religious background become so grounded in your faith that it is just as essential as breathing.

The Power of Refinancing
Refinance because your money depends on it!

One of the best choices I made was to eliminate debt. My student loans varied between 3-8% interest rates. Most of the loans were over 5%, and to be able to consolidate all these loans made for a better process overall. My goal was to tackle high interest loans first and then work my way down to lower interests. I refinanced based on who could get me the lowest interest rate. My first refinancing success with SoFi in 2017, I was able to get all loans above 5% down to 5%. That allowed me to see debt start to trickle away a bit faster. I was pleased with the progress being made, but still did some digging to see if I could lower it even more.

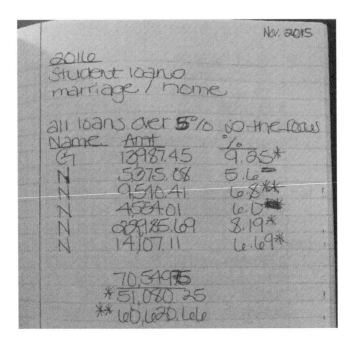

Figure 1: In 2015, strategizing only the high percentage loans to refinance

In 2018, I refinanced again with Georgia United Credit Union bringing my interest rate down to 3%! So far, I have not been able to find a better deal than that and used this outlet to chew away at student loan debt faster. I started to see the light at the end of the tunnel; nearing closer and closer. Because the rates were so low, I decided to make another sacrifice. Instead of paying once a month on the loan, I began to pay the loan twice a month. I did double-time each month to close out the life of the loan. Here I am, $0 later in student loan debt!

Refinancing is not a sexy process. This is adulting at its finest. Refinancing can be time-consuming because you have to search for the best options that work for you. Thankfully the options I found allowed consolidation of federal and private loans. Some refinance options do so by reviewing your credit score, some by your income and other ways. Find what works best for you. I encourage you to research other options online and locally and make a wise decision based on your circumstances.

REFLECTION
What did your budget plan reveal to you?
How will you manage overspending going forward?
What certifications or courses can you take to increase your skills and salary?
Faith without works is dead. What ways do you plan to increase your faith and change your mindset?
How will you remain consistent with your debt elimination plan?
What do you think about refinancing your loans?

seven
loan paid, now what?

It feels somewhat surreal to be done with student loan debt! It is also empowering to have my overall finances in order. Even as I write these words, it still feels like a dream. Like words I would never utter until I was old and grey. Well, I do have a few greys, but you know what I mean. The moment I made my last payment, I wanted the satisfaction of physically pressing the submit button for the payment. Usually, I had it on an automated method. However, a moment like this deserved a bit more attention. I had my husband record the entire process, I took screenshots, and danced like nobody was watching.

Dear NICOLE JONES:

Our records indicate that your Private Education Account listed above has a zero balance.If you authorized payment through your banking institution, please contact that facility to stop recurring payments. If you authorized payment through our web site, no action is needed.

Figure 2: Congratulations email from Georgia United Credit Union for completing the loan repayment process

Words really cannot describe the level of freedom I feel! What I thought would take me eons to eliminate was cut down by budgeting significantly.

When I thought I would be incompetent with money forever turned out to be a lesson of determination and will. When I thought generational poverty would curse me turned into breaking down the walls of comfort. When I thought I was going to make get-money-fast moves turned into mastering patience and strategy. When I thought God was punishing me turned out to be a lesson of obedience.

So, as you can tell the formula to financial success for me was all of these moments of transition, learning, and action. Understanding the root of my financial history, changing my mindset, owning up to my faults and seeking guidance, taking the necessary steps to activate change, and once accomplished help others also find their way. Now everyone's path will not be my path.

I want you too to accomplish the success of saying, I am financially free!

Break generational poverty
Debt-free feels like breaking the chain of societal restrictions. I want to share everything I have learned with family, friends and anyone willing to listen. There is no value in being debt-free without those around you being able to share that same sentiment. I want to utilize this new lease on financial freedom to uplift those around me also to succeed. When I think back to my parents who always instilled the importance of helping others, I find peace that the pages of this book aids in just that.

In my opinion, as a black person, systems are not made for us to succeed. Time and time again, we find ourselves working 10x harder than other counterparts. There are poorly funded schools in black communities. There are people who intentionally hold us back from success just because the color of our skin. Unfortunately, I cannot solve all world problems when it comes to injustice. However, I do have the power to use my platform to promote wealth and normalize it with anyone who identifies with facing financial struggles.

As black people, we must break the stigma of poverty. Support black businesses and allow funds to consistently circulate within our communities. As a community, we have to get in order. Individually, we have to practice self-advocacy. It is no easy task. Collectively, we have to change our mindsets and behavior in ways some of us have never learned. This book is my stepping stone in starting these conversations and for you to take action.

For some, making a financial transition will be uncomfortable and foreign. It may require tremendous sacrifice, which can be difficult if you are already struggling. Diamonds are created under pressure, and to see a change; you have to be the change. To see the results you want, it takes time, and that goes beyond just financial goals; that is with any goal. We have to unlearn poor money habits.

In a different light, some households perpetuate the beauty of struggle, which is another barrier we have to break. If you happen to be the highest income earner in your family, you sometimes feel bad. Why?

Some family members will, in turn, make you apprehensive to share good news because they are always struggling and would rather complain about life versus placing energy to improve their situation. Everyone faces hard times, but with the intent to actively do something about it, not live with a defeatist mentality. Some family will shame you in your success. You feel bad about doing well. Sounds crazy, I know, but this occurs in more family dynamics than you know. Misery loves company. Logically, it makes no sense, but this all goes back to breaking generational poverty.

We must provide the right tools for our families to thrive. If you are that person in the family who is doing well in your career, just know you are not the family ATM. There is nothing wrong with genuinely helping your loved ones in times of need. We all make strides to help our family. It is only when family members are riding on your coattails for constant financial gain does it become sticky. On the one hand, you love your family, and you want to help. On the other hand, if you say no, you feel bad because maybe you do have the money, but do not wish to continue to be a handout. Then guilt settles, you reflect on all they have done for you, they might even call and remind you of all they did for you, and then you fold. You are handing off more money. This is toxic emotional behavior. Without a doubt, your family means the world to you. By placing emotional ties as to why you should give them money is manipulation. There is nothing wrong with helping your family, but not because you were manipulated in doing so.

How can we help each other from constant financial struggles? Each person has to step up to the plate.

As mentioned, this will be a mindset and behavioral change. It will be taxing for anyone, but you have to want to change. Also, if you are the family ATM, consider alternative ways to help. Inquire about them joining you in an educational webinar about money management. Say something like; I do not have the funds right now to give because I just joined this financial course; would you like to join me? Find ways you can be a resource without having to give money all the time. You want to enable them to learn better money habits, not disable them always to ask. And finally, for any situation, share knowledge. Have more open conversations about money. Finding out historical knowledge about family may help you better understand the patterns and how to begin to chip away at generational issues.

I look forward to passing down knowledge and wealth to my future kids that will last throughout many generations. They will learn and understand the importance of generational wealth and continue to educate those that follow them. They will learn generational wealth is more than just money, but also how to sustain family legacy. They will learn generational wealth is a balance of finance, faith, philanthropy, and positive character.

Stack ya money & invest
There are a few things I have my focus on now: save, invest, and philanthropy. All three of these to-dos will never really stop throughout my life. Now I have more opportunities to increase in these areas. Greg and I have already started planning out what life after student loans looks like.

I should add another huge announcement here: Greg is also student loan debt free! This debt-free journey did not happen overnight; we planned for this. With a few obstacles along the way, we made it. God willing, all of our aspirations will come true.

I think the continuation of saving goes without explanation. I simply want to be secure, confident, and prepared for "life happens" moments. I am over feeling financially inadequate, living paycheck to paycheck, and stressed about money. Been there, done that. As for investments, this has many ways to make an appearance. There is so much I want to accomplish, and I look forward to sowing into different avenues. Investment ideas include real estate, entrepreneurship, and the stock market.

Real estate is something I have had an interest in literally since a little girl. I can vividly recall coming home from school watching home improvement shows and just being fascinated. Both Greg and I are learning more every day about the industry and sought out mentorship as well. This is new territory, and I know together we can succeed if we truly dedicate ourselves. I have several venture ideas and who else to fund those dreams than me. All bets on me! I encourage everyone to bet on yourself by investing in educational resources and guidance that will help you succeed.

Over the past few years, I have actively been playing in the stock market as another stream of income, one of the best decisions I FINALLY made.

I was one of those people who was always interested in the market because I heard it was an excellent avenue for income and boy, were they right.

Once I got over the procrastination is when I began to see results. Greg was pivotal in this journey of investments as he was already trading prior to us dating. So, he taught me the ropes, and now we challenge each other with daily trades. A healthy challenge, of course, but we try to one-up each other on daily gains. Every day in the market is not always a win, but there are substantial gains to be made. My goal is to continue to make smart trades and share what I have learned with others.

Giving back to the community and church was instilled in me at an early age. It was something that you do because if you have the means you help those who are less fortunate. Now I can make a more significant impact on the community. Philanthropy is a selfless act that does not require recognition or accolades. It is merely the satisfaction of helping others in need that rewards all of us. When it pertains to giving, that can include either time or money, or both. There are so many organizations in need, and I look forward to mapping out my wish list. Who knows, my husband and I may even start our foundation!

The opportunities are endless! I know I have a plan in mind, but God has something more magnificent. Throughout this journey, I had all the right people and tools to help me through this. However, nothing greater could have got me to this point without God.

It was in his design for me to take this trek, unlearn and learn again, and share this story. I am ready for my new financial journey to unfold. I am prepared to share my story with others so they, too, can conquer goals. I am stepping into debt-free life and learning new ways to grow.

As for you, I want the same debt free life for you. I want the same not just for you, but the generations that follow behind you. My hope is this journey and tools will be applied to your own life to become debt free!

REFLECTION
What would you do with your money once you paid off student loans?
What is the first thing you would invest in with the extra cash?
How would you give glory to God for this success?

FINANCIAL CONTRACT

Today, I, _____, on _____, _____ 20__, signs this contract to better my finances and challenge my determination. Starting today, I will no longer fold to debt and feel defeated by overdrawn accounts. I hold myself accountable for my actions and will rise to the occasion for the sake of my wellbeing and the generations that follow.

I agree that starting today; I no longer place blame or excuses on anyone regarding my finances because I am in control of my destiny. I will outline my shortcomings, create a monthly budget, and adhere to the necessary steps to achieve financial freedom. I will seek out financial guidance for those that are trained in this space to help further propel me. I owe it to myself to invest in myself. As I gain financial knowledge, I will share with those I know who are also in need and willing to listen. Ultimately, I have to be the change if I want to change to happen around me.

I acknowledge that financial freedom is in scope for me. I am capable and willing to become debt-free. I will remain prayerful and encouraged, even when up against signs of defeat.

I understand all these requirements and the journey in-between to see a positive change in my life and my bank account.

Signature: _____

REFERENCE

To further help you elevate your financial well-being download the **Mediocre to Masterful Financial Freedom Planner**.

This planner is for you if:

- You are tired of feeling frustrated with your finances
- You need a financial self-help guide
- You need more detailed steps on how to succeed
- You need affirmations to motivate you along the way
- You need a digital spreadsheet to get your finances in order

Use code **ACCESS** at check-out to download your discounted copy at mediocretomasterful.com.

REFERENCE

A copy of the full digital spreadsheet can be found in the **Mediocre to Masterful Financial Freedom Planner**.

Personal budget	Jan
INCOME	
Wages	0.00
Interest/dividends	0.00
Miscellaneous	0.00
Income totals	**0.00**
EXPENSES	
Home	
Mortgage/rent	0.00
Utilities	0.00
Home telephone	0.00
Cellular telephone	0.00
Home repairs	0.00
Home improvement	0.00
Home security	0.00
Garden supplies	0.00
Home totals	**0.00**

This planner will help you outline your entire budget and monthly expenses. You will be able to quickly identify what areas you need to scale back and where to you can save more money.

The more you know about your finances and become closely aligned with spending habits the better you will be at eliminating debt. Give this exercise your all!

Personal budget

	Jan	Feb	March	April	May	June	July	Aug	Sept	Oct	Nov	Dec
INCOME												
Wages	0.00	0.00	0.00	0.00	0.00	0.00	0.00	0.00	0.00	0.00	0.00	0.00
Interest/dividends	0.00	0.00	0.00	0.00	0.00	0.00	0.00	0.00	0.00	0.00	0.00	0.00
Miscellaneous	0.00	0.00	0.00	0.00	0.00	0.00	0.00	0.00	0.00	0.00	0.00	0.00
Income totals	0.00	0.00	0.00	0.00	0.00	0.00	0.00	0.00	0.00	0.00	0.00	0.00
EXPENSES												
Home												
Mortgage/rent	0.00	0.00	0.00	0.00	0.00	0.00	0.00	0.00	0.00	0.00	0.00	0.00
Utilities	0.00	0.00	0.00	0.00	0.00	0.00	0.00	0.00	0.00	0.00	0.00	0.00
Home telephone	0.00	0.00	0.00	0.00	0.00	0.00	0.00	0.00	0.00	0.00	0.00	0.00
Cellular telephone	0.00	0.00	0.00	0.00	0.00	0.00	0.00	0.00	0.00	0.00	0.00	0.00
Home repairs	0.00	0.00	0.00	0.00	0.00	0.00	0.00	0.00	0.00	0.00	0.00	0.00
Home improvement	0.00	0.00	0.00	0.00	0.00	0.00	0.00	0.00	0.00	0.00	0.00	0.00
Home security	0.00	0.00	0.00	0.00	0.00	0.00	0.00	0.00	0.00	0.00	0.00	0.00
Garden supplies	0.00	0.00	0.00	0.00	0.00	0.00	0.00	0.00	0.00	0.00	0.00	0.00
Home totals	0.00	0.00	0.00	0.00	0.00	0.00	0.00	0.00	0.00	0.00	0.00	0.00
Daily living												
Groceries	0.00	0.00	0.00	0.00	0.00	0.00	0.00	0.00	0.00	0.00	0.00	0.00
Child care	0.00	0.00	0.00	0.00	0.00	0.00	0.00	0.00	0.00	0.00	0.00	0.00
Dry cleaning	0.00	0.00	0.00	0.00	0.00	0.00	0.00	0.00	0.00	0.00	0.00	0.00
Dining out	0.00	0.00	0.00	0.00	0.00	0.00	0.00	0.00	0.00	0.00	0.00	0.00
Housecleaning service	0.00	0.00	0.00	0.00	0.00	0.00	0.00	0.00	0.00	0.00	0.00	0.00
Dog walker	0.00	0.00	0.00	0.00	0.00	0.00	0.00	0.00	0.00	0.00	0.00	0.00
Daily living totals	0.00	0.00	0.00	0.00	0.00	0.00	0.00	0.00	0.00	0.00	0.00	0.00

Made in the USA
Coppell, TX
13 May 2021

55588054R00026